ROSS PEROT

Billionaire Politician

—PEOPLE TO KNOW—

ROSS PEROT
Billionaire Politician

Carmen Bredeson

ENSLOW PUBLISHERS, INC.
44 Fadem Road   P.O. Box 38
Box 699   Aldershot
Springfield, N.J. 07081   Hants GU12 6BP
U.S.A.   U.K.

Library of Congress Cataloging-in-Publication Data

Bredeson, Carmen.
    Ross Perot: billionaire politician / Carmen Bredeson.
        p. cm. — (People to know)
    Includes bibliographical references and index.
    ISBN 0-89490-545-7
        1. Perot, H. Ross, 1930– —Juvenile literature. 2. Presidential
candidates—United States—Biography—Juvenile literature.
3. Businessmen—United States—Biography—Juvenile literature.
I. Title. II. Series.
E840.8.P427B74 1995
973.928'092—dc20   W 1922   94-27996
  [B]   CIP
                                AC

Printed in the United States of America

10 9 8 7 6 5 4 3 2 1

Illustration Credits: AP/World Wide Photos, pp. 6, 114; Courtesy of Ross
Perot, pp. 13, 15, 17, 22, 26, 29, 30, 32, 35, 36, 49, 52, 61, 63, 78, 83, 89,
99.

Cover Illustration: Courtesy of Ross Perot

Contents

Ross Perot

1

Election Night—1992

A smile as wide as Texas spread across the face of Ross Perot as he stood before the cheering crowd. People waved flags and clapped for the 1992 presidential candidate on this, the night of the election. Perot was on stage in the ballroom of the Grand Kempinski Hotel in Dallas, Texas. He was conceding the race to Bill Clinton, the new President-Elect.

As an independent candidate Ross Perot had received 19 percent of the votes cast in the election that day. Only one other third-party presidential candidate had amassed a higher total of popular votes. Teddy Roosevelt and his Progressive party received 27 percent of the vote in 1912.[1] Historically, third-party and independent candidates have had limited appeal, only winning the support of voters in their local areas.

What led to Ross Perot's success in 1992? One factor was that Perot, a billionaire, did not have to depend on contributions to run his campaign. He had unlimited funds at his disposal and the freedom to use the money in ways that he thought would be most effective. Another factor was that Perot used television to contact the American people, taking advantage of television's widespread audience. Through "infomercials," thirty-minute blocks of network time that he bought, Perot informed the public of his views.

Using charts and diagrams, he outlined his economic plan to reduce the deficit in terms that were easy to understand. He pointed out that the national debt in 1992 had risen to $4 trillion! He said that it would take $214 billion in 1993 just to pay the interest on that debt. He hammered away at the problems of excessive spending in Washington, D.C. He warned Americans, "Government is not a candy store in which every group can pick from any jar it wants. This is not free money. It's your money, and more importantly, it's your children's money."[2]

Instead of tuning out his "infomercials" for their favorite television shows, many American viewers watched Perot's programs. And they responded to them with letters and phone calls. The television time and other campaign expenses would eventually cost Ross Perot more than $60 million of his own money.

Meanwhile President Bush and Governor Clinton

financed their campaigns with money from the Presidential Election Campaign Fund. Each candidate was allocated $55.2 million in federal money to pay for his presidential bid.

A considerable number of Americans were ready for a candidate such as Perot. The United States government had gotten bigger and bigger throughout the years, and many people felt that their elected officials were no longer in touch with public opinion. Ross Perot said over and over in interviews that Washington should "listen to the people" and that "the people are the owners of this country."

He believed that whoever occupied the White House needed to pay attention to what American citizens were saying. A total of 19,097,214 voters responded to Perot's message. They went to the polls in droves to cast their vote for the Texas billionaire with the big ears and short haircut.

The Ross Perot who stood on the stage that November 3 in North Dallas did not appear to be saddened by his defeat. Rather he appeared elated that his message had gotten through to so many. He congratulated President-Elect Clinton for his victory in winning 43 percent of the votes. Perot said to his supporters: "The American people have spoken. They have chosen Governor Clinton. Congratulations."

When the crowd began to boo at Clinton's name, Ross Perot held up his hands, shook his head, and said,

"Wait a minute. The only way we are going to make it work is if we all team up together. So let's give Governor Clinton a big round of applause."[3] As the audience clapped, Perot nodded to the band and the musicians struck up his theme song "Crazy." Ross Perot turned to one of his four daughters, who was among the crowd of family members standing behind him. Then the two danced across the stage amid cheers and whistles.

Many events had happened in the life of Ross Perot since his birth on June 27, 1930, in Texarkana, Texas. Industrious and determined since childhood, the life of young Ross included such diverse activities as breaking horses at age eight, earning an Eagle Scout badge at age thirteen, and excelling as a member of the high school debate team. As a United States Naval Academy student he would twice be elected president of his class.

Those same leadership qualities of his youth had served him well during the often bumpy road of the 1992 election. Even though he had received a barrage of criticism and made some questionable decisions, many voters wanted Ross Perot as their President. The roomful of supporters gathered before him on election night certainly had confidence in his ability. What past experiences and influences had helped to shape Ross Perot into the successful grinning man who stood before the cheering crowd that night in Dallas?

2

Childhood

Gabriel Ross and Lulu May Perot were married in 1923 and then built a red brick house at 2901 Olive Street in Texarkana, Texas. Their first son, Gabriel Ross, Jr., was born two years after the couple married. He tragically died of spinal meningitis in 1927, when he was only a year and a half old. The Perots subsequently had a daughter Bette in 1928 and a son Henry Ross in 1930.

Gabriel Perot was a large man who was in the cotton wholesale business. He was well known around Texarkana for his charming personality and sense of humor. Lulu May was a kind woman who worked as a homemaker. The Perot couple was often seen holding hands and they liked to go dancing on Saturday night. During the rest of the week the two spent much of their free time with Ross and Bette.

The family usually ate dinner together in the evening. Perot remembers that fried chicken, spaghetti, pot roast, and chicken pie were among his favorite meals. After a big dinner the family liked to gather around the radio and listen to comedy shows or to President Franklin Roosevelt's "fireside chats." The weekly programs from Washington, D.C., were broadcast by the President to keep the American people informed about the state of the nation. When the weather was warm the family sat on their big front porch and visited with friends and neighbors. During those long summer evenings others came to 2901 Olive Street too—people who were strangers in town.

The time was one of massive unemployment in the United States, due to the effects of the Great Depression. Many businesses failed and jobs were lost after the collapse of the stock market in October 1929. Thousands of former wage earners were out of work and out of luck. Desperate, hungry men would sometimes quietly knock on the back door of the Perot house and ask to do some work in return for a meal. Lulu May helped as much as she could. She tried to keep a little extra food in the house to give to those who were in need.

Fortunately for the Perot family, the business of buying and selling cotton continued in spite of the Depression. Bette and Ross attended the Patty Hill Elementary School, a private school where classes were

Gabriel Ross Perot was in the business of buying and selling cotton in Texarkana. Despite the Great Depression, his business was successful.

small and discipline was strict. The children studied the usual subjects as well as the Bible, art, literature, and even Latin. The whole school participated in stage plays that were produced every year. Ross was a member of the band and played an accordion that was almost as big as he was.

There were a lot of rules to obey at the private school, and often the students were asked to recite a poem from memory at the beginning of the day. Even though the $7.00-per-student monthly tuition was high for the time, the Perots willingly paid it because they believed in the importance of a good education. Ross spent four years at the private school and then he transferred to the public school system in Texarkana.

Ross seemed to find plenty to do during the summer and on weekends. His favorite pets included a dog named Shep and a horse called Bee. According to the season, a neighborhood softball, football, or basketball game was usually easy to find. Friday night movies were an event that was anticipated all week long. On Sunday mornings the Perot family could normally be found at the Methodist church. They also enjoyed annual trips to the circus and state fairs. Sandwiched in between his school and social functions were all of the jobs young Ross did to earn money.

Across the street from the Perot house was an empty lot where the family kept a few horses. Ross learned to ride at a young age, and by the time he was eight years

Ross and Bette Perot attended the Patty Hill Elementary School in the mid-1930s.

old he was "breaking" horses for a dollar apiece. The horses that he was paid to "break" had never before been saddled and ridden. Sometimes Ross won and sometimes the horse won. The snorting bucking animals tried their best to throw the small boy—and a few succeeded! A broken nose or a concussion did not seem to deter young Ross though. He got right back on the big horses to try again. Gabriel and Lulu May raised their children to believe that they could do anything if they tried hard enough.

When Ross was twelve he went to the local newspaper, *The Texarkana Gazette,* to see about getting a paper route. At that time the price of a weekly subscription to the *Gazette* was twenty-five cents. The delivery boy got to keep a little over a nickel of the amount collected from each subscriber. All of the routes were taken, but Ross made a unique proposal to the management.

Ross proposed that he would deliver the paper to the two poorest neighborhoods of Texarkana, New Town and Avondale. But he wanted more than double the regular commission to do so. No one else had bothered to try selling papers in Avondale or New Town because most of the residents there were so poor. Also a few rough characters lived in the two areas, and some people were afraid to venture into the neighborhoods.

The *Gazette* agreed to give Ross a try, and the small boy set out on his horse to sell subscriptions. In spite of

Lulu May and Gabriel Ross Perot instilled in their son a sense that he could do anything if he tried hard enough. It is a philosophy that Ross has adhered to throughout his life.

the fact that they had very little money, many of the people Ross approached responded enthusiastically to the idea of having a newspaper delivered to their homes. Ross ended up selling many copies of the *Texarkana Gazette*, eventually making $25–$30 a week.[1]

After seeing how successful young Ross was, someone in the circulation department of the newspaper tried to reduce his commission. Ross went straight to the paper's publisher and said that an agreement had been made and he didn't think it was fair for the rules to change just because he was doing better than expected. The publisher agreed with the convincing young boy, and Ross continued to be paid at more than twice the going rate for his subscriptions.

During the time he was delivering papers, Ross also got involved in the Boy Scouts. He joined the Flaming Arrow Patrol in 1941, and through hard work, made Eagle Scout just eighteen months later. In 1970, when he was forty years old, Ross Perot said, "The day I made Eagle Scout was more important to me than the day I discovered I was a billionaire."[2]

His old scoutmaster Sam Shuman remembers Ross Perot as "a small boy, a very friendly chap. He was always pretty well self-sustained and had good leadership ability."[3]

As news of World War II began to dominate the airwaves, the Perot family often turned on the radio to listen to the latest bulletins from overseas. They heard disturbing reports about the Germans' relentless advance throughout Europe. The United States managed to stay out of the fighting until December 7, 1941. Then, on that day, the Japanese launched their surprise attack on the American fleet stationed at Pearl Harbor, Hawaii.

More than 3,000 people died and many ships were destroyed or damaged in the early Sunday morning attack. The nation listened as President Franklin Roosevelt described that day as a "date which will live in infamy."[4] Congress then declared war on Japan. Within a short time Germany also declared war on the United States. America was suddenly thrust into the middle of World War II.

By the summer of 1942, eight million Americans were overseas. Back home in towns such as Texarkana, there were air raid drills and blackouts. And there was always news of the staggering number of casualties. After just a little more than one year, 60,000 American soldiers had been killed in battle.

The Perot family, like millions of other American families, listened to the grim news and did what they could to support the war effort. Many women took jobs in factories, because the men who usually worked in the industrial plants were serving overseas in the armed forces. Men who were left behind because of old age or poor health tried to help keep the country running.

With the Boy Scouts, Ross collected used books to send to the troops.

There was a great feeling of patriotism in the United States during World War II. Perot's lifelong sense of patriotism probably began to develop during these years when all Americans were urged to pull together for the good of the country. Ross listened while neighbors gathered to talk about the war and the heroic efforts of the American fighting forces. A sense of pride in his country would remain with him throughout the years—far past the days when the war finally ended.

By May 7, 1945, Germany had been defeated and the war in Europe was over. The war with Japan raged on until the United States dropped an atomic bomb on Hiroshima on August 6, 1945, and another on Nagasaki two days later. The Japanese finally surrendered, and World War II ended on August 14, 1945. More than 600,000 American soldiers had died while fighting for freedom.

After the battles finally stopped, life in cities and towns across the country slowly began to return to normal. People put their lives back together and tried hard to forget. But many had unforgettable images of the terrible tragedy that would never entirely fade. Young Ross also stored his war memories in his mind—memories that would influence him for the rest of his life.

When World War II ended in 1945, Ross Perot was fifteen years old. As the rest of the country returned to peacetime activities, so did Ross and his friends. As a high school student he was involved in typical teenaged activities.

He remembers that algebra and government were among his favorite subjects in school. For recreation he swam, and was a lifeguard at the Texarkana Country Club. Since he was too small to play football or basketball, he took up tennis. He practiced often and hard so that he could beat his friends when they played against him.

Ross earned good grades in school and stayed out of trouble. Unfortunately he saw less and less of some friends as they discovered alcohol. Ross promised his father that he would not drink or smoke, and he kept his promise. As his high school years came to an end, Ross dreamed of attending the United States Naval Academy in Annapolis, Maryland. He wrote many letters of application, but they were not answered. At that point he decided to attend Texarkana Junior College.

Ross Perot quickly got involved in campus life and began to make a name for himself. He discovered that the school yearbook, *The Bulldog*, had not been published for about sixteen years. Ross organized a staff and together they worked hard to publish a yearbook.

Ross Perot enjoyed many activities as a teenager in Texarkana, among which was horseback riding.

He later became involved in a plan to move the growing school to a larger lot across the street.

Perot decided that the limited amount of space in the proposed location would not provide enough room for the school's growth. Instead he suggested that the campus move to an eighty-eight-acre tract of land that was located on the west side of Texarkana. Years later his English teacher Claude Pinkerton said, "It was incredible. He had covered every angle. He had maps, graphs, tables, charts—everything. He had done economic feasibility studies, he had spoken to other junior colleges about growth."[5]

Eventually after the administrators heard all of Perot's arguments and looked at his evidence, they agreed with him and took his advice. The school campus was relocated and has grown comfortably during the past forty-five years. The other students began to recognize that Ross was something of a leader. They elected him president of the Texarkana Junior College student council in 1948. Professor Pinkerton remembers that one day in class he said, "Ross, you could be President of the United States if you desired."

Ross replied, "Mr. Pinkerton, that wouldn't be bad, would it?"[6]

In 1949 Perot's dream of attending the United States Naval Academy finally came true. Senator W. Lee O'Daniel of Texas was retiring. As he was going through the papers in his Washington, D.C., office, O'Daniel found that there was still one appointment to the Naval Academy that could be filled by a Texas student. When he asked if anyone was interested, his aide replied that there was a young man from Texarkana who had been writing letters of application for years. The senator had never met or heard of Ross Perot, but he said to give the appointment to him.

3

The Navy Years

On June 27, 1949, which was the day of his nineteenth birthday, Ross Perot was sworn in as a midshipman at the United States Naval Academy in Annapolis, Maryland. Freshmen at the Academy were called plebes, or middies, and every minute of their lives was regimented. They marched to class, to the dining hall, and to the dorms. Their appearance had to conform to military regulations and their rooms had to pass strict inspections. Perot, who was organized even as a child, thrived in the structured atmosphere of the Naval Academy.

Perot had participated in debates all during his high school and junior college years. When he was still an unknown plebe at the Naval Academy, he used some of his previous experience to get some recognition. During

Ross Perot, a midshipman at the U.S. Naval Academy in 1950, stands
on the deck of the USS *Roan*.

a September debate competition "he did a superb job" according to one of his classmates. Arlis Simmons added, "The whole class knew who he was. That's really how he got started."[1]

Even though Perot earned only average grades in his academic subjects, his ability to handle himself well in a variety of situations was soon recognized. He was appointed battalion commander and was always ranked near the top of the leadership lists. He was also elected to be vice president of his sophomore class, and during his junior and senior years, he served as class president. In addition to Perot's success at school, another important event occurred during his last year at the Naval Academy.

On October 18, 1952, Ross Perot met eighteen-year-old Margot Birmingham. A blind date for the couple had been arranged by mutual friends. The two met in a popular restaurant near the campus. According to Ross, "It was love at first sight; it still is, every time I lay eyes on her."[2]

Margot later said, "I just loved being with him. I couldn't wait to go out with him again."[3]

When she met Ross, Margot was a sophomore at Goucher College, a women's school in Towson, Maryland. She was studying sociology and anthropology. She had grown up in Pittsburgh, Pennsylvania, the youngest of Donald and Gertrude Birmingham's five daughters.

Ross and Margot had many dates during Perot's senior year at the Naval Academy. As graduation day approached for Perot, the prospect of a long separation faced the young couple. Since his education at the academy had been paid for by the Navy, Ross was required to serve four years of active duty in return. Shortly after graduation he was scheduled to leave for a year-long cruise.

Graduation day arrived and so did Mr. and Mrs. Perot and Ross' sister, Bette. Margot was already in the area so she joined the Perot family to watch as Ross was awarded his diploma. When all of the festivities were over, and before he left for the ship, Ross gave his Navy ring to Margot to wear in his absence. They promised to write long letters to each other.

Perot's birthday once again was the occasion of an important day in his life. Twenty-three-year-old Ensign Ross Perot reported for duty aboard the destroyer USS *Sigourney* on June 27, 1953. Originally the ship was destined for the waters off Korea, to provide support for the American troops then engaged in the Korean War. The United States military had come to the aid of South Korea in 1950 when that country was invaded by communist-supported North Korea.

By 1953 when Perot's ship was ordered to the area, the Korean War had reached a stalemate. A truce was declared and the fighting ended, but not before more than 23,300 Americans had been killed in battle. Since

Ross Perot's leadership abilities were recognized at the U.S. Naval Academy. Here Perot is congratulated by Admiral C. Turner Joy.

Ross Perot, with his parents and sister, Bette, at his graduation from the United States Naval Academy in 1953. Shortly after his graduation, Perot served aboard the destroyer, USS *Sigourney*.

the *Sigourney* was no longer needed for war duty, it was given new orders. Perot and his shipmates spent the next year cruising around the world's oceans and visiting dozens of foreign ports.

The destroyer was a part of the American Naval fleet that was sent to various locations around the globe. In the event that trouble occurred in distant ports, ships that were cruising in nearby waters could respond quickly. During the long hours at sea Ensign Perot wrote many letters to Margot. He wrote about his travels and his feelings and his work in the Navy.

Shore patrol was one of Perot's duties while he served aboard the *Sigourney*. Many of the ship's 300 sailors got carried away when they were finally able to go ashore after weeks at sea. Ensign Perot often had to break up fights and haul some of his drunken shipmates out of bars and back to the ship before it was due to set sail again. Though he did not drink, Ross got the challenging job of corralling many of those who did.

As he spent more time in the Navy, Perot became dissatisfied with the Navy's promotion methods. It seemed that seniority was the only criteria used to decide who would advance in rank. Perot felt that hard work and merit made little difference, and that only the number of years served seemed to matter. This was a difficult system for Perot to accept. All of his life he had been action-oriented, liking to see tasks done quickly. In later years he would say, "The waiting in line concept

Perot's years at Annapolis prepared him for his responsibilities in the Navy. As an ensign aboard the USS *Sigourney*, Perot travelled extensively and visited many foreign ports.

was just sort of incompatible with my desire to be measured and judged by what I could produce."[4]

Perot's problems seemed to increase when a new captain was assigned to the *Sigourney*. Soon after, Perot asked for a transfer to a different ship. In 1955 Perot was reassigned to the aircraft carrier USS *Leyte*. He began seeking an early release from active duty and a transfer into the Naval Reserves. He had decided that a military career was not for him and he wanted to leave the Navy as soon as possible. Perot enlisted the help of his father, who sent letters to Texas Senators Lyndon Johnson and Price Daniel, Sr.

The elder Perot wrote that "inasmuch as we are not in war at this time and the Navy is just training a young officer who desires to be released I was wondering if you could assist us in this matter through the Secretary of the Navy."[5] The requests were denied and then, late in 1955, Gabriel Ross Perot died in Texarkana. After the death of his father, Perot abandoned his appeal for an early release from duty.

When Margot Birmingham found out about the death of Gabriel Perot, she left for Texarkana to attend the funeral. Margot was a recent college graduate and had been teaching third grade at a private boy's school in Baltimore, Maryland. The arrival of Margot during this very difficult time meant a lot to Ross. Her sympathy and caring were evident as the young couple was reunited. Before Ross reported back to his ship, they had set a date for their wedding.

During a brief leave from the Navy, Henry Ross Perot and Margot Birmingham were married in the First Presbyterian Church in Greensburg, Pennsylvania. The large afternoon wedding on September 15, 1956, was attended by about 300 guests. After the ceremony a reception followed at the country club.

On that memorable day Ross wore his white Navy uniform and Margot wore a traditional long white wedding dress and veil. After a brief honeymoon the young Mr. and Mrs. Perot moved to Wickford, Rhode Island. This is where Ross was stationed at the Quonset Naval Air Station.

The newlyweds lived in a small apartment. Margot taught school while Ross spent much of his time at sea. Years later Margot said that theirs was a traditional marriage from the beginning. "Material things were never very important to us. They still aren't. We could go back to that first year and be just as happy as we are now. As long as I'm with him, I don't care."[6]

One day, aboard the *Leyte*, Ross had a conversation with a Naval Reserve officer who was an executive with International Business Machines (IBM). At that time the IBM corporation was a pioneer in the new high-tech world of computers. The man suggested that Ross might like to apply for a job with the company that had been founded in 1924.

On September 15, 1956, Henry Ross Perot and Margot Birmingham were married at the First Presbyterian Church in Greensburg, Pennsylvania.

Ross and Margot Perot on their honeymoon in 1956.

Since his four-year obligation to the Navy was almost completed, Perot decided to look into the job. He took the IBM aptitude tests and passed. In 1957 Lieutenant Perot was honorably discharged from the U.S. Navy and was on his way in the world of business.

4

IBM

During the summer of 1957 twenty-seven-year-old Ross Perot and his wife, Margot, put their few belongings in their 1952 Plymouth and drove to Dallas, Texas. Perot had a job waiting for him at IBM, a company that in the beginning he really knew very little about.

The Perots found a duplex house and rented the downstairs apartment. To lower the monthly rent to $110, Ross took care of the yard and did some maintenance work around the place. While Ross attended training sessions and familiarized himself with IBM, Margot taught fourth grade. She stopped teaching when the couple's first child, Ross, Jr., was born in 1958.

Ross Perot seemed to fit right in at IBM. All of the salespeople had to wear conservative clothing and keep their hair neatly trimmed. He said, "When I went to the Naval Academy I got a short haircut and liked it. It's efficient. You don't have to waste time combing it."[1] The orderly atmosphere at IBM also appealed to the organized Perot.

As he began his career Perot told one of the company's managers, "Sir, I know you pay higher commissions for new business and tough accounts. So give me your toughest accounts."[2] Ross Perot quickly became the top salesperson at IBM.

He sold the 1401 model, a huge machine the size of a refrigerator. It had a very limited memory capability and could hold only about four pages of an average book. Today even a small laptop computer can hold a large amount of data.[3] For businesses at the time though, the 1401 model meant a radical new approach to data processing. Slow and limited as they were, early computers could do the work of several employees. The machines also eliminated a lot of unnecessary paperwork and filing.

Computers were a relatively new product on the market. In 1946 IBM had introduced a machine that contained 18,000 vacuum tubes and weighed thirty tons. The IBM machine could add, multiply, divide, and calculate square roots at up to 5,000 steps a second.[4]

The rapid advance of technology during the 1950s soon led to the development of the transistor, a dime-sized device that eventually replaced many of the bulky vacuum tubes. Then, in 1954, IBM introduced an all-transistor calculator that did not contain any vacuum tubes at all. As technology continued to advance, scientists learned how to make transistors and other electronic components smaller and smaller.

The introduction of the microchip during the 1970s brought a real revolution to the computer industry. Usually made of silicon, one nickel-sized chip could do the work of 100,000 dime-sized transistors. The huge computers of the past gave way to compact machines that easily fit on a single desk or even in one's lap. Modern computers can do millions of operations a second.

When Ross Perot began his career in the computer industry, the machines were not only quite large, they were a mystery to most American businesspeople. Perot's job was to convince companies that a computer was just what they needed, and he did his job very well. Instead of getting a monthly salary, Perot worked on commission and received a percentage of each sale that he made. Before long Perot was making more money than some of the company's managers. It was then that IBM began a new policy that put a limit on the amount of commission a salesperson could earn.

Perot usually worked long hours and did not waste a lot of time eating lunch and taking coffee breaks. By January 19 he had already met his 1962 sales quota. He had made all of the money allowed for that year, and technically, he didn't have to do any additional work because he wouldn't be paid any more salary. Instead of just wasting his time though, he continued to try to devise new ways for the company to earn profits.

At that time IBM sold just computer hardware; the computer program's software was given to the customer for free. The trouble was, no one outside IBM had any idea how to program the machines. Once a sale had been made, an IBM salesperson's job was actually just beginning. Long training sessions were held to teach the customer's employees to use the computers. Also, the software had to be designed to fit the needs of each individual business, because standardized software did not exist in the early days of the computer industry. An IBM salesperson was always on call to answer questions and to help program his customer's computers.

Ross Perot suggested to the IBM management that they should sell an entire computer package. He wanted the package to include machines, trained staff to run them, and software designed to fit that particular customer's needs. When IBM rejected his idea, Perot began to question his future with the company. He had already demonstrated that he could successfully sell computers, but was prevented from making any additional money that year. IBM's rules stood in Perot's way just as the Navy's promotion methods had frustrated him.

One day as he sat in a barber shop waiting to get his

weekly short haircut, Perot picked up a copy of *Reader's Digest*. As he looked through the magazine, he happened to see a quotation by Henry David Thoreau, a nineteenth-century poet/philosopher. It read: "The mass of men lead lives of quiet desperation." Perot realized that he was stuck in just that kind of predicament and had nowhere to go with IBM. He decided that maybe it was time to strike out on his own and market his ideas.

5

EDS

Ross Perot founded Electronic Data Systems (EDS) on June 27, 1962, just seven weeks after he read the Thoreau quotation. In order to incorporate and begin the business, he had to pay a $1,000 state incorporation fee. Since he couldn't find any investors to back the company, in the beginning Perot's wife, mother, and sister were on the original board of directors. Perot said in later years, "We really lived very modestly. I had never bought a new car. We didn't own a washing machine, and we had saved our money."[1]

Financially the family was doing well when Perot decided to leave IBM. He had already made his full commission from the computer company during January. He also had a part-time job processing claims for Blue Cross-Blue Shield, a private insurance firm. In order to have space for his new business, Perot rented an empty office from Blue Cross and hired a secretary. After he finished his daily work for the insurance company, he made phone calls and tried to promote the services of EDS.

The big selling point that Perot stressed to potential clients was the fact that EDS would take care of everything connected with the computer. His staff, when he had a staff, would operate and maintain the machines and design software to fit the customer's needs. The customer only had to provide the raw data and EDS would do the rest. In the dawn of the computer age, full-service computer operations were very appealing. Few people knew anything about the new technology and were intimidated by the complicated machines.

But in the beginning, business was very slow for EDS. During the first four months, Perot made over seventy sales calls before he signed his first contract. Then in February 1963, Perot got his first big break when the Frito-Lay Company agreed to pay $5,128 per month for data-processing services. Perot said "I used odd numbers like $5,128 in those days to make it look like I knew exactly what I was doing and had figured everything down to the last penny."[2]

Business began to pick up, and by spring, EDS had seven employees, each of whom spent very long hours at the office. One afternoon Ross Perot left the office and didn't tell anyone where he was going. When he returned later in the day, he admitted that he had been to see each of the spouses of his staff members. He wanted to apologize for the long working hours and give each family 100 shares of EDS stock even though "it wasn't much of a gift." Those same shares were worth $200,000 by 1986.[3]

Perot's own responsibilities at home increased with the addition of daughter Nancy, who was born in 1960. His parents had included Ross and Bette in most of their activities and he, too, wanted to be a part of his children's lives. Perot was committed to his marriage and his children, and he expected EDS employees to feel the same way about their families.

He said, "If we have a married employee who has a girlfriend, we terminate him. He's got a lifetime contract with his wife, and if she can't trust him, how can I? It's that simple."[4] Even though his rules were extreme and legally unenforceable in most states, his employees seemed to accept them as a part of the job.

Ross Perot had very definite preferences when it came to the kind of people he hired to work at EDS. He said, "I wanted people who are smart, tough, self-reliant, have a history of success since childhood, of being the best at what they've done, people who love to win."[5] He employed mostly military veterans, requiring them to wear white shirts with dark suits and keep their hair cut short. These were the rules of Perot's former employer, IBM. Women staff members were also expected to dress conservatively and they could not wear pants except on very cold days.

Perot expected his people to be dedicated and committed to making EDS the best computer company around. There was not an executive dining room or special parking places for company officers. Everyone ate together in the same cafeteria and drove their own cars to work. Limousines had no place at EDS. Perot always tried to find the best person for each job, in spite of that employee's position in the company. The EDS symbol was an eagle, and the company motto was "Eagles don't flock; you have to find them one at a time."

Electronic Data Systems continued with the pattern of slow but steady growth. As the contracts increased, additional employees were hired. There were company picnics and a Christmas banquet every year. If an employee had medical or personal problems, Perot tried to help in whatever way he could. During his brief free hours at home, Perot enjoyed the activities of his growing family. A second daughter named Suzanne was born to Ross and Margot in 1964.

In 1965, with health costs out of control, many older Americans and people with low incomes could no longer afford to visit doctors or be hospitalized. That year the U.S. Congress passed into law the Medicare/Medicaid bill. Medicare would provide government assistance and supplementary insurance to those over sixty-five. Medicaid, operated by state governments and insurance

Perot employed the best people he could find for each job at EDS.
Here he is pictured with (from left to right) Tom Marquez, Tom
Walter, and Mitch Hart.

agencies, was designed for younger people who did not have enough money to pay for medical care.

No one predicted just how many Americans would be eligible for the two public assistance programs that President Lyndon Johnson signed into law. After Medicare and Medicaid were established, the flood of patients who qualified for federal assistance far outnumbered the estimates.

Insurance companies such as Blue Cross-Blue Shield were suddenly flooded with thousands of claims to process. There were not enough employees to handle the staggering workload. Insurance companies all across the country experienced the same problems. Several forms had to be completed for each patient before the government-subsidized healthcare payments could be collected. There were not enough hours in the day to complete all of the work.

Because he was a part-time employee of Blue Cross, Ross Perot knew how to process claims. He also saw firsthand the effects Medicare had on insurance companies. EDS, with its trained computer operators and data processing ability, was the perfect solution to a growing problem.

Perot soon had the contract to handle the Texas Blue Cross claims, and before long, he had signed contracts to handle Medicare claims in several other states. Perot was in the right place at the right time. His firm was selling a product that many were clamoring to buy. Other companies sold computers capable of processing the claims, but EDS offered trained staff members who knew how to do the work.

As new business poured in, EDS struggled to keep up with the increased demand. By 1968 more than 300 people were employed by Ross Perot. It was time to sit back and take a look at the future. Up until now all of the stock in EDS was owned by the employees and the Perot family. Maybe the time had arrived to offer the public an opportunity to buy into EDS. This could be done by offering to sell shares of EDS on the New York Stock Exchange. And the public offering would help the company expand even more rapidly. The decision was a difficult one for Perot because every share that was purchased represented an outside part-owner of the company. He would no longer be totally in control of his company.

Finally on September 12, 1968, Perot made the decision to list EDS on the New York Stock Exchange. EDS stock opened its first day of trading at $16.50 a share. By the end of the day its price had risen to $23.00. Before 1968 ended the stock listed for $160 and would eventually be sold for $200 a share, making Ross Perot suddenly worth almost $2 billion dollars![6] And the company was just seven years old.

Ross Perot's life didn't change dramatically as a result of his new-found immense wealth. The family remained in its four-bedroom home in North Dallas,

With his new-found wealth, Perot purchased his childhood home in
Texarkana and had it carefully restored to its original appearance.

and Perot's salary stayed at $68,000 a year—the same amount that he made before EDS went public. What did change was the amount of free time he had to spend on matters unrelated to the office.

One of the first ways he spent some of his money was to buy the house in Texarkana where he was raised. Perot had many happy memories of his childhood and wanted to preserve the house where he spent his younger years. Lulu May Perot had been a widow since 1955, and had sold the house during the mid-1960s. At that time she moved to Dallas to be closer to her son and his growing family.

The new owners at 2901 Olive Street had covered the red brick exterior of the Texarkana house with white paint. After the owners moved, Perot tried to have the paint removed so that the house would look like it did when he was a boy. The crew he hired tried various methods of paint removal, but they failed to restore the bricks to their original red color.

Undaunted, Perot asked the crew to chip away the grout that held the bricks in place. Then each brick was turned around so that the unpainted side faced out, and then cemented back into place. It was a huge job, but eventually the transformation was completed and the house was restored to its original appearance. Today it remains empty, but is very carefully tended by a hired caretaker.

6

Vietnam and Beyond

Like many other people who lived in the United States during the 1960s, Ross Perot was interested in the Vietnam War and the ever increasing buildup of American troops in Indochina. The war was being fought to try to stop communist North Vietnam from occupying noncommunist South Vietnam. The United States became involved because many believed that the fall of South Vietnam would lead to further communist takeovers in Indochina, and eventually, in the rest of the world. The perceived spread of communism, country by country, was known as the "domino theory."

During the 1960s U.S. involvement in the war increased dramatically as the years passed. Early in the decade President John Kennedy sent American troops to advise and help train South Vietnamese soldiers. Later,

President Lyndon Johnson assigned troops to combat roles in Vietnam. By the mid-1960s there were about 150,000 American soldiers in Vietnam. The number quickly rose to half a million by the end of the decade.

Throughout those years many American soldiers and pilots were injured and killed, while others were taken prisoner by the communist forces. As many as 2,000 American men were either classified as prisoners of war (POWs) or were listed as missing in action (MIAs). The few who escaped from the North Vietnamese prison camps reported that conditions there were terrible.

Often the men were kept in solitary confinement in tiny rooms and were routinely tortured by their captors. They were fed only enough to keep them alive. Medical treatment was not available for injuries that were sustained during capture, so broken bones and wounds went untreated. In addition, most of the cells contained loudspeakers so that communist propaganda could be played day and night for the weak and starving Americans.

In 1969 Ross Perot decided to use some of his new wealth to try to improve conditions for the American POWs in North Vietnam. He arranged to lease two 707 jet airplanes so that he could fly Christmas dinner, gifts, letters, and medicine to the POWs. He and his crews loaded tons of food and supplies aboard the two planes and took off for Hanoi. His requests to deliver the goods were repeatedly denied by the North Vietnamese government, and Perot and his volunteers had to return home.

Instead of giving up, however, he made another attempt three months later in March 1970. Again he leased two planes that he called "Peace on Earth" and "Goodwill Toward Men." On the second trip he took along five women whose husbands were being held prisoner as well as nearly a hundred reporters. Again Perot's requests were denied by the communist government, and none of the supplies made it into American hands. The disappointed people in Perot's group stopped in Laos and stood outside of the North Vietnamese embassy to protest the poor treatment of the POWs.

During the same months in 1969 Ross Perot founded an organization called United We Stand. He spent $1 million on newspaper and television advertisements that were aired to inform the public of the plight of the POWs. He also wanted to try to gain support for President Richard Nixon's Vietnam policies.

When asked in 1969 what he hoped to get for all of the money he had spent, Perot replied, "Not political power or elective office. I'm too action-oriented, which means if I had an idea on Friday and wanted it done by Monday it would be just too much to expect from government."[1] Instead, Perot wanted to inform the public about the Nixon plan and the POW and MIA issues.

In an attempt to extract the United States from the unpopular war, President Nixon had initiated a program that he called Vietnamization. It called for the gradual withdrawal of American troops so that eventually the South Vietnamese army could take over all of the combat roles. Perot agreed with this plan. In the United States there was a growing public outcry because many people believed that the troop withdrawal was not being accomplished quickly enough.

Many Americans were tired of seeing rising casualty figures on the evening news. College campuses became the sites of huge anti-war demonstrations. Protest marches were a common sight in Washington, D.C. Some men who were opposed to the war burned their draft cards or fled to Canada to avoid being drafted into the armed forces. "Flower children" and "hippies" proclaimed love and peace. Some turned to drugs to escape reality. America was being torn apart by a war that very few believed in or supported anymore.

Eventually—after many years of involvement—all of the American troops were withdrawn from Vietnam, but not before 58,000 had died in the fighting. In 1973 a U.S. cease-fire agreement with North Vietnam ended America's role in the Vietnam War. The agreement also stipulated that, in exchange for our troop withdrawal, all American POWs had to be returned. Gradually the weak and starving men were flown home to their loved ones in America.

Once home in the United States, and after a period of adjustment, some of the former POWs began to talk about their years in captivity. Many of them said that the attempts Ross Perot made to deliver Christmas gifts to them did have a positive effect on their treatment. The publicity surrounding those trips brought the plight of the prisoners before the whole world. Pressure from the outside affected the North Vietnamese, and they gradually allowed more mail to get through and gave the prisoners food that was a little more nourishing.[2]

On April 30, 1975, the Vietnam War officially ended when South Vietnam unconditionally surrendered to the communists. The war eventually cost the United States the lives of nearly 60,000 men and more than $140 billion.[3] Questions about the 2,000 men who are still listed as missing in action continue to haunt the families who were left without any answers. Those missing men have never been forgotten by Ross Perot either, and he continues to mount searches and inquiries about them to this day.

After the turbulent years of the 1960s, the beginning of the early 1970s started out to be calm enough. But the tranquility didn't last long. Ross Perot, the recent billionaire, decided to set up a charitable foundation in order to spread his wealth. He asked his sister Bette to run the foundation for him and to help decide which organizations needed aid the most. One of his first donations was a $2.4 million grant for a school to educate underprivileged African-American and Mexican-American children in Dallas.

Perot had good memories about his days in scouting. He gave the Boy Scouts $1 million so that the organization could try to establish some troops in low-income neighborhoods. The Girl Scouts also received a ranch from Perot, to use as a boarding school for disadvantaged girls. The New York City Police Department even received a gift of sixteen Tennessee walking horses and saddles for their mounted police unit—replacements that the department couldn't otherwise afford.

When he wasn't sifting through the hundreds of requests for money that poured into his Dallas office every day, Ross Perot was catching up on life at home. During the early years of EDS, he had spent long days at the office, getting his new business running smoothly. Now that there was no question of the success of EDS, he turned the day-to-day operation of the company over to a business partner and had more time to devote to his family.

By 1971 there were five Perot children. Ross, Jr., was thirteen; followed by eleven-year-old Nancy. Then came Suzanne, age seven, and Carolyn, age three. Last of all was baby Katherine. The family had finally outgrown their four-bedroom house and had moved into a lovely new home on a twenty-two-acre estate in north Dallas. Stately white columns stretched across the front of the

Ross Perot enjoys spending time with his family. Here he is shown with his son, Ross, Jr.

Perots' red brick house. It was surrounded by acres of beautiful lawns and gardens, and had stables for several horses.

Ross Perot had never gotten over his fondness for horses and riding. He often took his various offspring along when he rode around the property. The little ones, who were still too small to handle a horse, rode on the saddle in front of their dad. When the young Perots got bigger and were more skilled in the saddle, they were allowed to ride alone.

One day while the children were playing, Suzanne's dog ran away. Heartbroken and in tears, she went to her father for help. Dad immediately took control of the situation and began to make signs that described the lost dog. He then got on his bicycle and put up the signs all over the neighborhood. Before long someone called to say that the dog had been found. Ross Perot never liked to sit around and wait for something to happen when he could be taking action himself.

The 2,000 American servicemen who were still missing from the Vietnam War were people whom Ross Perot never forgot. He wanted those men accounted for so that their families could stop wondering about the fate of their loved ones. In 1973 Perot's concern prompted him to pay for a spy network that searched for missing Americans.[4] The next year Perot financed a secret mission into Laos that was led by Colonel "Bull" Simons, a retired army officer and Green Beret.[5]

Ross Perot with Katherine, the youngest of his five children.

Unfortunately neither trip turned up any of the missing Americans.

In 1973 Ross Perot was warned by the Federal Bureau of Investigation (FBI) that, because of his covert MIA searches, he was a target for assassination by the North Vietnamese. He immediately hired an extensive security force to guard his home and family. Inside the tall stone wall that surrounds the Perot estate, there are still armed men and guard dogs that patrol the grounds twenty-four hours a day.[6]

Some trouble also developed at the office in 1974, when EDS came under government scrutiny. There was a congressional investigation into the company's extensive contracts to process Medicare and Medicaid claims. Federal auditors wanted to examine the books at EDS to see if the company made excessive profits. Perot said that the government was free to look at the accounts that pertained to Medicare and Medicaid. However he refused to allow them to see the accounts of any other EDS business that was not related to those programs. The auditors continued to insist that they be allowed to look at *all* of the company's financial records.

Medicaid specialist Wesley Amend said about the dispute, "While this dumb game goes on, the programs are suffering. The thing that's wrong with Perot isn't that he's providing bad service or that he's overcharging.

It's the way he churns everything up and submerges the whole thing in controversy."[7]

When Perot was asked about the work his staff did for the government insurance carriers, he said, "My people painted a Rembrandt and now they're being criticized by people who couldn't whitewash a fence."[8].

7

Iranian Rescue

The controversy of the congressional investigation didn't seem to hurt business at EDS. In 1976 the company signed a $20.5 million contract with the government of Iran, a country that is located along the Persian Gulf in the Middle East. EDS agreed to set up a social security and health insurance program for the country's thirty-three million citizens. Perot sent dozens of employees to install a computer system that was needed to process the mountains of information. Many of the EDS employees were accompanied by their wives and children, who planned to live in Iran while the project was carried out.

Several months after the arrival of the Americans, a revolution to overthrow the ruler of Iran began to ferment. The ruler of Iran, called the Shah, had been in power for more than thirty-five years. Gradually over the next year and a half, the forces that opposed the Shah gained strength. By 1978 the situation had gotten ugly, and massive demonstrations were common in the streets of the Iranian capital of Tehran. Supporters of the exiled religious leader, Ayatollah Khomeini, wanted him to replace the Shah as ruler of Iran. Armed mobs roamed the streets shouting "death to the Shah."

Conditions continued to deteriorate and Perot feared for the safety of his employees. He decided to evacuate most of them, especially the women and children. A small team of company officials stayed behind to look after the equipment owned by EDS and to continue with the project. Bad news arrived on the afternoon of December 28, 1978. Ross Perot got the phone call during a family vacation at Vail, Colorado.

Two EDS employees, William Gaylord and Paul Chiapparone, had been arrested and put into a Tehran prison. The government of Iran was asking $12,750,000 for their bail—the amount that the government had already paid EDS for the computer work. Ross Perot immediately left for Dallas so that he could make arrangements to get his men back.

He contacted many officials in Washington, D.C., and tried to arrange for the release of his men through diplomatic channels. When all of the calls to Washington proved to be futile, Perot took matters into his own hands. He called sixty-year-old Colonel Arthur

"Bull" Simons and asked him to help free the men. Simons had searched for MIAs in Vietnam for Perot a few years earlier and was a respected and tough leader. The former Green Beret agreed to lead the commando raid and immediately packed to go to Dallas.

In the meantime Perot put the word out for volunteers among his own employees. He was looking for men who were former combat veterans. Perot said, "I told each man that I was about to discuss something with him that could cost him his life, and if, for any reason, he should not be involved, our discussion should go no further. Every man I talked with volunteered."[1]

Simons arrived and began to plan the raid with twelve EDS men. They ordered supplies and equipment and began to train physically for the upcoming rescue. Conditions continued to deteriorate in Iran, and the Shah fled his homeland on January 16, 1979. As the training continued in Dallas, Perot decided to personally go to Iran to see the two imprisoned EDS employees. Before he left, though, he went to the hospital to talk to his mother who was dying of cancer. She agreed that there was a great deal of danger connected with the plan, but she said, "You don't have a choice, Ross. They're your men. You sent them over there. They didn't do anything wrong."[2]

Shortly after this mother-son talk Perot left for Iran. He used his own passport and even signed in at the jail with his own name. Apparently the name of Ross Perot meant little to the custom officials or the prison guards. The guards led Chiapparone and Gaylord from their cell to a meeting room. The two men did not have any idea who their visitor might be and were amazed to see their boss, in person, standing in the Iranian prison. After an emotional greeting Bill Gaylord and Paul Chiapparone gratefully accepted the packages of warm clothing, food, and medicine that Perot brought to them. The letters and messages from their loved ones at home were also very much appreciated.

During Perot's visit he warned his men to be ready for an escape in the near future and advised them to go to a certain hotel in Tehran when they were free. Ross Perot also carefully examined the jail so that he could report back to Colonel Simons. He found Gasr prison to be heavily fortified, surrounded by twelve-foot walls and guarded by men with automatic weapons.

Perot and Simons later agreed that it would be nearly impossible to break into the structure. Instead Simons and his men would try to incite a mob to storm the prison and demand the release of the 11,800 inmates.

On February 11, 1979, there was a massive demonstration in the street in front of the jail. An armed mob fired on the gates at Gasr prison until the locks were destroyed. Fearing for their lives, the guards abandoned their posts and fled into the streets. Then the crowd stormed the prison and unlocked the cells one by one. Unfortunately, among the 11,000 prisoners who escaped were murderers and rapists who were once again free to prey on the Iranian people.

After just seven weeks of imprisonment, the two EDS employees escaped during the confusion that followed the riot. As gunfire erupted around them, Gaylord and Chiapparone carefully picked their way through the dangerous streets. They made it to the Tehran hotel where Colonel Simons and his men were waiting. After a warm reunion, plans were made for the last leg of the escape. Two all-terrain vehicles were bought and supplied for the two-day, five-hundred-mile journey to the border of Turkey and final freedom. The group couldn't travel safely by air because a bulletin had gone out about the two escaped Americans, and officials were looking for them.

The final leg of their escape was touch and go. Colonel Simons and the EDS men were led through the countryside by an Iranian accomplice, who had been an employee in the EDS office in Tehran. The ragged looking team was stopped often during its trek, and carefully searched and questioned. In each terrifying instance they were finally allowed to pass.

On February 15, 1979, all of the men involved in the raid safely stepped across the Turkish border. Perot was nervously waiting in Istanbul. From there he and the group of men flew home in a leased Boeing 707. When the group arrived in Dallas a crowd of family members and EDS employees was waiting to welcome home the tired but happy men.

A State Department spokesman in Washington, D.C., later said, "All we know is that the prison was stormed or collapsed that weekend. There was no U.S. government involvement in anything Perot did. We had no knowledge that he was taking his people out of Iran."[3]

Cyrus Vance, Secretary of State in the Carter Administration, said, "The privatization of foreign policy is a dangerous matter." Vance then went on to say that he "was troubled by that mission."[4]

Less than two months after the successful raid, Lulu May Perot died in Dallas. Soon after that, on May 21, 1979—a little more than three months after he led Perot's men to safety—Colonel Arthur Simons died. The author Ken Follett later wrote about the daring rescue in a best-selling book titled *On Wings of Eagles*. Also a five-hour television mini-series was made about the harrowing experiences that EDS employees had in Iran.

Other American hostages who were taken prisoner in Iran were not as fortunate as the EDS employees. Iranian supporters of the Ayatollah Khomeini were angry that the deposed Shah had been allowed to enter the United States to get medical treatment. They wanted him to stand trial in Iran. In an attempt to force the return of the Shah, militants stormed the American embassy in

Tehran on November 4, 1979, and took sixty-six employees hostage. A few of the hostages were later released, but fifty-two remained in the hands of their captors.

A rescue attempt ordered by President Jimmy Carter on April 28, 1979, failed. Several helicopters full of commandos were sent to Iran, but they were recalled after one of the aircraft crashed, killing eight American servicemen. The hostages were finally released on January 20, 1981, after 444 days of captivity.

8

New Ventures

In 1979 Texas Governor William Clements asked Ross Perot to chair a committee to examine the problem of illegal drugs in the state. Since Perot had recently appointed Morton Myerson as chairman of EDS, he had some extra time that he could devote to the issue. Governor Clements was concerned about the growing drug traffic between Texas and Mexico. He wanted the War on Drugs Committee to discover ways to halt the spread of illegal narcotics at the border and he picked the well-known Perot to head up the project.

Perot thought that the panel should address all of the drug problems in Texas and arranged for experts to come and talk to the group. He also traveled around the state and appealed to parents, students, and teachers to join in the war on drugs.

Ross Perot and former Vietnam POW, General Robinson Risner, went to Washington, D.C., to ask First Lady Nancy Reagan to join in the fight against illegal narcotics. She agreed that drugs were a serious threat to society and later began a nationwide "Just Say No" program to try to educate children about the dangers of illegal drugs.[1] Perot spent more than $1 million of his own money to study the issue. He and his eleven-member committee proposed a series of bills to the Texas legislature that were designed to make it harder for illegal drug sales to take place in the Lone Star state.

After some discussion and a few minor changes, the legislature passed all of the bills that were recommended by Perot's committee. New laws were enacted that legalized the use of wiretaps in drug investigations and allowed the police to seize the property of convicted drug dealers. Mandatory life sentences were proposed for adults who were found guilty of selling drugs to minors. Also, a program was begun in Texas that attempted to educate school children about the dangers of using narcotics.

Perot's work with the anti-drug campaign prompted another Texas governor to ask for Perot's help. Mark White had been elected to replace Bill Clements, and during his campaign, Governor White promised to pay the state's public school teachers higher salaries. In 1984 he asked Ross Perot to head up a committee that would discover ways to raise revenues to pay for the wage increases.

In his usual manner, Perot tackled the entire education system instead. Using his own money he traveled to school districts around the state and visited with administrators, teachers, students, and parents. The committee listened to experts and looked at possible solutions to some of the problems that existed in the Texas school system.

Perot and his fellow committee members discovered the existence of several problems that prevented Texas education from being the best that it could be. Perot said that "we've been through 25 years of fads in education—new math, new alphabet, new style of reading—whatever some professor could come up with. Out of that we produced a generation of children who cain't [sic] figure, cain't read, cain't spell."[2]

The Governor's Task Force on Education made several recommendations that were presented as bills before the Texas legislature. One called for fewer students per classroom in the elementary grades and additional Head Start programs for children from low-income families.

The sentiments that Perot expressed concerning children and poverty in 1984 were not very different from the ones he expressed in an interview nearly ten years later. He said, "If I could have one wish for our schools in this country, it would be to get severely

The father of five, Perot's concern for children and the educational system in Texas was apparent. Perot's children (clockwise): Ross Jr., Nancy, Katherine, Carolyn, and Suzanne.

disadvantaged children into school shortly after birth. It would cost a fraction of what it costs to put them in jail or keep them on welfare, and they become productive, successful, taxpaying citizens."[3]

Perot and his committee also found huge differences between rich and poor school districts when it came to funding. The committee advised that reform was needed to make the allotment of state money equal among all of the districts in Texas.

Another area of concern revolved around public school teachers. The vast majority were wonderful qualified educators, but occasionally a few bad ones had slipped through the cracks. The task force recommended that all Texas teachers be required to take an exam to prove that they were competent to teach school. That request produced an outcry from teacher's groups around the state. Eventually the test was given to all Texas teachers and only a small percentage failed to pass the competency exam.

Probably the most controversial recommendation that the committee made involved athletics. A bill was presented that would prohibit an athlete from taking part in extracurricular activities, including sports, for a period of time if he or she failed an academic course. In a football-obsessed state such as Texas, that rule could knock some of the best players right out of competition. In addition, the panel wanted to raise the passing grade from 60 to 70, thereby making it even tougher to pass.

In spite of the groans of protest from coaches around the state, most of the bills were passed by the Texas legislature. They were enacted into law and accompanied by higher taxes to pay for their sweeping reforms. Charles Beard, who was then the president of the Texas State Teacher's Association, went to Beaumont, Texas, to hear Perot speak at Lamar University. After the speech, Beard stated: "The guy said everything I wanted to hear. So much of it we had been trying to make happen for a long, long time."[4]

As his work with the education system wound down, Ross Perot was presented with a new challenge. General Motors, the biggest corporation in the world with more than 800,000 employees, had been steadily slipping in the new car market. Early in the 1980s, GM sold 46 percent of the cars that Americans bought. By the end of the decade the auto giant only had a 35 percent share of the market.[5] GM, founded in 1908, had been an industry leader that had employed 200,000 workers in 1936. The worried directors were scrambling to recapture their lost customers and their lost revenues. They looked to EDS for help.

Perhaps a merger with the high-tech Electronic Data Systems could help streamline the computer side of General Motors and make the entire business enterprise more efficient and cost effective. After a great deal of negotiation, GM bought EDS on June 27, 1984, Perot's fifty-fourth birthday. The 45,000-member EDS work force was part of the $2.5 billion deal. Ross Perot became a member of the board of directors at General Motors and was the company's largest stockholder, with his 11.3 million shares of GM stock.

When asked why he sold the company that he had spent so long developing, Perot said, "I didn't need the money. The only reason I sold EDS to GM was because I couldn't think of anything more interesting to do with the rest of my life than to help revitalize the biggest corporation in the world."[6] With his usual energy Perot began to learn about General Motors from the inside and the outside. He visited manufacturing plants and car dealerships. He talked to the assembly-line workers and company managers. He asked the buying public what kind of cars they drove and why. After all of his inquiries he concluded that the corporation had gotten so big that it had lost touch with the customers and the employees alike.

It cost General Motors more to build cars than any of its major competitors spent on producing their automobiles. He blamed GM's problems on the fact that each new idea that surfaced was studied in depth before a decision was made. He said that at EDS, the "first EDSer to see a snake kills it. At GM, first thing you do is organize a committee on snakes. Then you bring in a consultant who knows a lot about snakes. Third thing you do is talk about it for a year."[7]

Perot began to criticize the company openly as he

became more and more frustrated with the slow pace of change at GM. He said that trying to get GM to modify its business practices was "like teaching an elephant to tap dance."[8] Comments such as that finally wore out the patience of Roger Smith, president of GM, as well as the good humor of the board of directors. In 1986 a meeting was held that Perot did not attend. At that meeting members of the GM board decided to buy Perot's 11.3 million shares at twice the market rate. They planned to offer Perot a total of $700 million to leave General Motors.

Later a person present in the negotiations said, "Ross could never accept the fact that he had sold EDS and would not be able to maintain the level of autonomy that he was used to." Roger Smith later said of the buyout that Perot "is a different type of guy than we are in GM. He is impatient."[9]

As part of the $700 million deal, Ross Perot agreed not to criticize GM in the future or be fined $7.5 million if he did.[10] He also promised not to compete with his old company, EDS, for eighteen months. One day past the year and a half deadline, Ross Perot founded Perot Systems.

The year 1988 proved to be a busy one for Ross Perot. Perot's new company, like EDS, was a computer services business. From his seventeenth floor office on Merit Drive in Dallas, Ross directed his new enterprise. Many collectibles that Perot had acquired over the years

Perot sits in his office in Dallas, Texas surrounded by family photos and memorabilia which he calls, "Ross's stuff."

were used to decorate the large office. He called all of his memorabilia "Ross's stuff."

Scattered on the walls were original Norman Rockwell paintings that depicted everyday American scenes in such an extraordinary manner. Some of Frederick Remington's wonderful western bronze sculptures were displayed on tables and shelves, along with eagles of all sizes and descriptions. On the wall behind Perot's desk was the famous painting, "Spirit of 76." Pictures of his wife and children filled the remaining empty spaces.

Before long the new company's client list began to grow, and Perot was back in business. As he grew older and his list of accomplishments increased, public speculation naturally surfaced about a career for Ross Perot in the world of politics. When questioned about his political aspirations, he continued to deny that he had any interest in holding an elected office.

In 1988 he stated that "my mother used to say—Ross, a little bit of you goes a long way. I guess quite a few people today would agree. That's why I'd be no good at politics in this laid-back cool world of television."[11] But in less than five years, Ross Perot would throw his hat into the ring in his bid for the office of President of the United States.

9

Candidate Perot?

On February 20, 1992, Ross and Margot Perot traveled to Washington, D.C. Margot stayed behind in the hotel room while her husband went to a television studio to appear on CNN's *Larry King Live* show. After nearly an hour of King's leading questions about a possible presidential bid, Perot finally agreed that he might be willing to run as an independent. But first he said that volunteers had to circulate petitions and get his name on the ballot in all fifty states in time to meet the filing deadline. Back at the hotel Margot Perot was stunned as she watched the program. She later said, "It was such a surprise to me. I don't think Ross thought he would say it himself."[1]

Perot's decision unleashed a massive volunteer effort that involved thousands of people. No one, not even

Perot himself, could have imagined the eruption of support that followed his announcement. People wore "Ross for Boss" and "Run, Ross, Run" T-shirts to rallies that were being held in many cities and towns. Armies of interested Americans circulated petitions in all fifty states. And one by one the petitions were returned, filled with the names of people who were willing to sign on the dotted line for Ross Perot.

The momentum continued to grow as dissatisfied Americans lined up to support Perot. His followers believed that government had gotten too big; it no longer represented the wishes of the American public. The national debt was too huge to even imagine, yet Washington continued to spend and spend and tax and tax. Many people were looking for an alternative to the Democratic and Republican candidates. Maybe an independent such as Ross Perot was the answer.

Third parties have appeared from time to time in American politics. In 1854 the two major political parties in the United States were the Democrats and the Whigs. Even though slavery was an important issue at that time, neither party was willing to take a position concerning freedom for all people. The Republican party was organized as part of an anti-slavery movement. Abraham Lincoln was the first of many Republicans elected to the presidency, and the Whigs eventually disappeared.

Ross Perot's March announcement that he would

run for President caused speculation about the formation of a possible third party. The Democratic Party had chosen Arkansas Governor Bill Clinton as its candidate. The incumbent Republican President George Bush was in the race to try and win a second term in office. The entrance of a third party could take votes away from either of these two contenders.

Back in Dallas after the talk show, the office phone lines were swamped with calls from media people who wanted to interview Perot, and from interested Americans who volunteered to help in the campaign. Perot rented some office space nearby and hired a small staff to handle the influx of requests. As the number of phone calls increased, hundreds of phone lines were installed and more were needed every day. In one ten-day period in March 1992, the office got more than one million calls! The enormous response was out of control. Ross Perot asked his long-time attorney Tom Luce to help develop an organizational plan. He looked to the leaders of successful past campaigns for help in his own run for office.

Democrat Hamilton Jordan and Republican Edward Rollins, both experienced political campaigners, were signed on as co-chairpersons of the Perot effort. Both men decided to abandon their former party affiliations in order to support Perot. Jordan said, "I believe that the possibilities of a Perot presidency are more promising and compelling than the certainties of a Clinton or Bush presidency."[2]

Rollins was even more complimentary when he stated, "I am convinced that Perot can provide strong presidential leadership and that he can end the gridlock in Washington. He is an honest moral man who believes in creating economic growth, jobs, and opportunity for average Americans."[3]

Once again everything that Ross Perot touched seemed to turn to gold. His life was one long success story, and now he had a chance to attain the highest office in the land. He had nearly everything that a human being could possibly want.

Perot was blessed with a lovely wife of thirty-five years, five grown children, and six grandchildren. Perot said that "five out of my five kids are too good to be true, thanks to their mother. She is a world-class mother."[4]

There were ample opportunities for entertainment at the Perots' home. The family members could bowl in the basement bowling alley or work out in the gym. Inside the Dallas mansion, the walls were lined with original paintings by Margot's favorite impressionist painters. Outside there was a swimming pool, tennis and badminton courts, and several horses to ride.

Or if they got tired of Dallas, the Perots might fly in their helicopter to a nearby getaway at Lake Texoma—where Ross kept his fleet of speed boats. For

Ross Perot, a proud father and grandfather, embraces his four daughters.

Christmas and Easter the family traditionally gathered at their ski chalet in Aspen, Colorado. And to really get away, the Perots could fly on one of their two private jets to their island paradise in Bermuda, where their yacht *Chateau Margaux* was moored.

Ross Perot's responsibilities at Perot Systems had decreased since Morton Myerson was appointed chairman of the company in 1991. Myerson, formerly EDS chairman since 1979, had stepped down when GM bought that company. After a five-year hiatus he was back at the helm of Perot's new company. Three of Perot's children—Ross, Jr., Nancy, and Carolyn—also worked for their father's company. Suzanne lived in New York, and Katherine was a college student.

Ross Perot continued as chairman of the board and still went to his office every day, but he didn't have to. Myerson had been with Perot since the 1960s and was certainly able to run the company. Ross Perot never had to work another day in his life if he didn't want to. What could have convinced him to give up the good life and propel himself into the harsh glare of a political campaign?

10

On the Campaign Trail

Ross Perot, Jr., once said that "a lot of guys would have climbed one mountain and quit. If my father doesn't have a challenge, he starts getting restless."[1] Maybe it was for the challenge that Perot embarked on the campaign trail. Ever since his experience at GM, he had been giving speeches about the gradual decline of America's manufacturing industry.

In 1987 he said that "we have unfairly blamed the American worker for the poor quality of our products. The unsatisfactory quality . . . is the result of poor design and engineering—not poor assembly. . . . The problem is a failure of leadership."[2] One of his speeches at the National Governor's Association was so successful that the chairman suggested Perot should run for President.

The chairman was Bill Clinton, then governor of Arkansas.[3]

To many people the problems of government were not very different from the problems in industry. Many elected officials no longer seemed to hear the voice of the people. Costs were out of control and many wanted some accountability from the leaders of the country. Where was the money going and was it necessary to spend so much? The national debt had risen from $256 billion in 1950 to $4 trillion in 1992. It continued to go up at the staggering rate of nearly $12,000 a second.[4]

The federal government had gotten more and more involved in everyday life in this country. In order to meet the increased demand for services, extra federal employees were continually hired and additional funds were appropriated to pay for the increases. During the Kennedy Administration 375 people were on the White House staff. In 1992 that staff numbered 1,850.[5] All branches of government had grown in a similar fashion and many of the voters wanted the runaway spending to stop.

Ross Perot appealed to the people who had given up on the traditional two-party system. Many of them had not even voted recently because they were unhappy with the choices on the ballot. Perot seemed to be an alternative to the status quo—a maverick who wasn't afraid to speak up about government waste.

The earliest petition deadline belonged to Perot's

home state of Texas. By May 11, 1992, 54,000 signatures were needed to put his name on the ballot in Texas as an independent candidate for President. On that warm spring day a crowd of supporters staged a parade and rally at the State Capitol in Austin. They handed in their completed petitions with 225,000 signatures—four times the number needed. Perot said to the gathered supporters, "Everyone that's an expert on politics said it would take six months to organize the nation state by state. From the bottom up, all of you across this country did it in five weeks. Not bad."[6]

By the time June 1992 arrived, a *Newsweek* poll showed that Ross Perot had a 35 percent share of the national vote. As his popularity rose, the press began to take his candidacy seriously and started to ask probing questions about the independent from Texas. Where did he stand on issues such as health care, the budget, and the decline of America's cities? How would he fix the current problems in each of those areas, and what about crime and the drug problem?

Perot said that he would study each issue carefully and consult with experts to develop specific recommendations for each of the serious problems that faced America. He was routinely criticized in the media for failing to provide specific solutions to America's problems.

As the days in June passed, the momentum that had begun just three months before continued to gather speed at an alarming rate. Hamilton Jordan and Edward Rollins were getting frustrated because a definite strategy for the campaign had not been mapped out. Both men had run successful presidential campaigns in the past, and they knew that the negative publicity that Perot was getting in the press every day had to be countered with positive messages.

Rollins and Jordan were ready to do a publicity blitz for their candidate, complete with television advertisements and political messages in newspapers and magazines. Perot objected to the amount of money the ads were going to cost and vetoed the plans. Since Perot was accustomed to writing his own speeches and making his own appointments, he disliked being "handled" by anyone. Rollins and Jordan began to wonder why they had been hired and talked about leaving the campaign. The negative publicity began to take its toll, and by July Perot's support had dropped to 26 percent.

As tensions grew and his supporters slowly faded away, Perot began to question the whole overwhelming series of events. One day, while he was having a conversation with Ed Rollins, Perot asked, "Is it ever gonna get fun again?"

Rollins questioned, "Fun?"

"Yeah. When I started, this thing was fun."

"Campaigns are never fun. It's like war."

"What about the presidency? Is that fun?"

"The only time the presidency is fun is the day you get inaugurated and the day you dedicate your library."[7]

The glare of publicity and the enormity of the situation began to affect Perot. He was very concerned about the safety of his family members and their loss of privacy. It seemed that negative articles about Perot were a daily feature in most magazines and newspapers. He was also repeatedly asked to give specific details about how he would streamline the federal government.

When he appeared on television's *Meet the Press* in the spring of 1992, Ross Perot was asked to explain how he planned to save the U.S. government a projected $180 billion a year. He replied, "This is an interesting game we're playing today. It would have been nice if you would have told me you wanted to talk about this, and I'd have had all my facts with me."[8] As his answers got more and more vague, Perot's numbers began to fall steadily.

On July 15 Ed Rollins resigned from the Perot campaign. That evening Ross Perot had a meeting with his family and closest advisors and the next day, July 16, he dropped out of the presidential race. He said he was afraid that in a three-way race, no one candidate would get a majority of the 538 electoral votes. In that event the House of Representatives would have to select the President and the Senate would be responsible for selecting the vice president. Perot felt that if such a situation occurred, it would disrupt the country.

As soon as the announcement was made, a cry of disbelief rose from thousands of Perot volunteers across the nation. A *Time/CNN* poll, taken shortly after Perot's withdrawal, revealed that 62 percent of his supporters felt that he had let them down.[9] Perot's public believed in him, and had worked hard to get his petitions filled with signatures. Hundreds of little mirrors arrived in Perot's mail. They were sent by angry supporters who asked their former candidate to take a look at himself. Perot was called a "quitter" by many in the press.

Phone lines in Dallas were jammed with calls—some from irate volunteers and others from those who said they wouldn't take "No" for an answer. They intended to file the petitions on the deadlines in spite of Perot's withdrawal. His name would appear on the ballot whether he liked it or not. He encouraged the volunteers to stay organized and continued to pump money into the campaign.

A few weeks after his withdrawal, Ross Perot appeared on the CBS television news program *60 Minutes*. At that time, he revealed the real reason he withdrew from the presidential race. Perot said that he quit because of information he received that his daughter's August wedding would be disrupted by the Republicans if he remained a candidate. Rather than take a chance of that happening, Perot said that he decided to end his candidacy.

A *Newsweek* poll following the broadcast showed

that only 26 percent of those questioned believed that a Republican plot actually existed. Marlin Fitzwater, a spokesman for President George Bush, called Perot a "paranoid person who has delusions and who seems to have latched onto this theory much like other people latch onto UFO theories."[10]

By August, Ross Perot's newly released book *United We Stand* was on the bookstore shelves. It quickly rose to the top of *The New York Times* best-seller list, where it remained for fifteen weeks. In spite of his withdrawal from the race, people were still interested in what Perot had to say about the gridlock in government. It began to look like Ross Perot would once again become a candidate.

Sure enough, on October 1, Perot re-entered the race. The volunteers had continued with their petition drives and had done a superb job. Ross Perot's name was on the ballot in all fifty states. The media speculated endlessly about who Perot would hurt most—President Bush or Governor Clinton? And what about the three upcoming debates? Would Ross Perot be allowed to participate?

Not only did he participate in the debates, he won a few new supporters as a result of his strong performance and humorous retorts. When questioned about his lack of experience in government Perot replied, "Well, they've got a point. I don't have any experience running up a $4 trillion debt." And in defense of his proposed

$.50-per-gallon tax hike, the candidate with ample ears said: "If there's a fairer way, I'm all ears."[11] In all three of his appearances Perot continued to hammer away about the serious effects the deficit was having on the country.

In addition to the debates, Perot was also spreading his views around the country via thirty-minute television infomercials and various public appearances. He talked about many of the topics addressed in his book. He said again and again that the federal deficit was $4 trillion and that every single day, the debt increased by another $1 billion. To help pay down the debt Perot said that all branches of the government needed to reduce their spending by 10 percent. He also advocated a number of new taxes that could be used only to reduce the deficit and not to provide additional money for expanded programs.

Some of Perot's proposals included a higher tax on cigarettes and social security benefits, and a ten-cent-per-gallon tax on gasoline each year for five years. Higher gas prices would raise revenue and also benefit the environment, because less fuel would be used due to its higher cost. On the other hand people such as those in the trucking industry, who depended on gasoline to make a living, would suffer financially from Perot's plan to increase gas taxes.

In *United We Stand* Perot also advocated the elimination of the electoral college. He said that the people should be allowed to vote directly for their choice

Ross Perot with wife, Margot. During his campaign, Perot spread his views around the country via television infomercials and public appearances.

for President. In the days before instant communication, the authors of the Constitution believed that the general public was not well enough informed to select the best candidate for the important job of President. Therefore they recommended that knowledgeable representatives of the people, called electors, be allowed to make the selection.

Today every state has the same number of electors as it has elected representatives in Washington. The electors are chosen at state conventions to represent that state's interests in the elective procedure. If the Republican presidential candidate gets a majority of the state's popular vote, then all of that state's electoral votes are supposed to go to the Republican. Likewise if the Democratic candidate wins the popular vote, the electors usually cast all of their votes for the Democrat— regardless of their own personal party affiliations.

Under this system it is possible for a candidate to get a majority of the popular vote, and yet lose the election because he or she did not amass enough electoral votes to win. In an era when most of the American people are much better informed than their predecessors, the electoral college seems to some to be an obsolete holdover from the past.

Holding elections on Tuesday also seemed a bad idea according to Perot. If elections were held on Saturday or Sunday instead, it would be easier for working people to vote and larger numbers might turn out to cast their ballots. Currently, polling places are open from 7:00 A.M. until 7:00 P.M. on election day. In some cases people are not able to get off work during those hours to vote.

From the beginning of Ross Perot's foray into the world of politics in March, he had encouraged a greater participation by the "owners of the country." Electronic "Town Hall Meetings" might be one way for citizens to make their wishes known to the Administration. Televisions could be specially equipped with devices that allowed people to vote on issues from their living rooms. Or toll-free phone lines could be made available so that viewers would have a way to vote on important issues that were discussed during the televised meetings. If every adult citizen in America were able to vote on issues from the comfort of his or her own home, maybe Washington, D.C., could better measure the desires of the people.

The idea of a nationwide method of instant communication was not as futuristic as it sounded. Fiber optic cables were already beginning to crisscross America. By 1996 home viewers in about 400 communities would be able to voice their opinions instantly through television hookups.[12] As more cable is laid, more cities and towns will be added to the network.

Another method of measuring voter approval or disapproval is already in place in Colorado. In many shopping malls and public buildings, there are computers that allow residents to express opinions about matters that are being considered by the government of the state. In *United We Stand* Perot said that "our political system can only be repaired if we take charge of it." He advocated greater participation in government by all American people—whether they supported him or not.

The third and final presidential debate was watched by an estimated ninety million television viewers. A record number of people were registered to vote. Some had not bothered to go to the polls in years. As election day approached political analysts bounced from one prediction to another. In the end, though, the voters held all the power.

11

After the Election

On November 3, 1992, 54 percent of America's 189,000,000 registered voters made a trip to the polls to vote for their presidential choice. When the numbers were all tallied, Arkansas Governor Bill Clinton was the winner with 43 percent of the total. President George Bush followed with a 38 percent share, while Ross Perot garnered 19 percent of the votes cast.[1]

Perot was clearly the loser in the race, since he carried no states and amassed no electoral votes. Yet on election night he hardly presented the picture of a disappointed failure. Instead he collected his considerable family around him in Dallas and seemed to be having the time of his life.

As his supporters cheered, he teased them by saying, "Is this the end? Or is it just the beginning?"[2] Clearly,

Perot must have had the nineteen million people who voted for him on his mind. What did the future hold for those disgruntled Americans, now that their candidate had lost the race?

After the election many Republicans and Democrats alike hoped that Ross Perot would get on his horse and quietly ride into the Texas sunset. Members of both parties eagerly lined up to welcome Perot's nineteen million former supporters into their respective groups. But Perot didn't seem to be going away.

On January 11, 1993, before President-Elect Clinton had even taken office, Perot founded an organization called United We Stand, America (UWSA) that had no relationship to the 1969 group of the same name. In its first twenty-four hours approximately 75,000 people joined. A brochure was mailed to solicit memberships. In it Perot said that the nonprofit organization was "dedicated to bringing about the necessary reforms in our nation's economy, government and election laws." For those who paid the $15 annual fee, a steady stream of newsletters and surveys would arrive in the mail during the following months.

As United We Stand, America gained members, Ross Perot began to once again buy television time to inform viewers of his stance concerning various issues. In a March 21, 1993, appearance called "The First National Referendum," he reminded voters of the need for government reform. A television infomercial followed on

April 25, 1993, in which Perot recalled the famous words of Thomas Jefferson who said, "I place economy among the first and most important virtues and public debt as the greatest of the dangers to be feared."

By the end of April 1993, just three months after President Clinton took office, a *Newsweek* poll showed startling new figures. When asked who they would vote for if the election were held today, 26 percent of those polled said that Ross Perot would be their choice. And a *U.S. News & World Report* poll showed Perot running neck and neck with President Clinton—with 35 percent of the vote for each man. Suddenly the Democrats sat up and took notice of the wily Texan, as did the 1996 Republican front runners.

No longer were Perot's comments and criticisms ignored. A special White House staff member was assigned the duty of examining the words of Ross Perot in order to weigh their significance. Senators and congresspeople began to meet and discuss issues with Perot. Was he lining up for a presidential run in 1996? If so, which party would he hurt most?

Another infomercial, called "The Tax Increase," was aired to protest President Clinton's proposed budget. Perot urged the viewers to contact the White House or their congressperson if they were dissatisfied with the President's plan. Telephone company sources reported that one million telephone call attempts were made to the White House switchboard during the forty-eight hours after the show aired.[3]

Phone calls in general have increased dramatically during the present Administration. During the years that former President Ronald Reagan was in office, the White House received about 5,000 calls a day. In 1993, at the beginning of the Clinton Administration, the number of calls rose to 40,000 a day.[4]

Perot wrote another book titled *Not for Sale at Any Price*, which zoomed onto *The New York Times* best-seller list in just two short weeks and stayed there for twelve weeks. In the forward of the book he said, "It's time to pick up the shovel and clean out the barn! Let's get to work." In *Not for Sale at Any Price* Perot offered solutions to the growing federal deficit. He once again said that increased gasoline taxes were one way to collect extra revenue and pay down the debt.

He also addressed the fact that half of the annual federal budget, or $728 billion, is spent on programs such as Social Security, Medicare, and welfare payments. Next in order of dollars spent is national defense, with an annual budget of $298 billion. And third is interest on the debt, at $199 billion a year. Perot pointed out that for the first two massive expenditures, people are helped and the country is protected. But for the $199 billion spent on interest payments, the country gets no return on its investment.

During the summer of 1993, UWSA members were

urged to organize. Volunteer groups that had no formal structure during the pre-election petition drives, began to elect officials. State conventions were planned so that bylaws and constitutions could be written. Each local nonprofit chapter would be licensed by UWSA and would be free to examine both state and national issues. In the UWSA newsletter that arrived in the summer of 1993, Ross Perot urged his supporters to get involved.

Often, when Perot appears on a television talk show, he is asked how many people belong to UWSA. He laughs and replies that the number will be revealed at the right time, but no later than December 31, 1993. Then he continues to talk about the latest issue on his agenda.[5] The last day of 1993 passed without any revelation about the total membership of UWSA.

12

NAFTA, Health Care, and the Future

An issue on Ross Perot's mind during the summer and fall of 1993, was the North American Free Trade Agreement (NAFTA). The pact proposed gradually eliminating trade barriers that existed among Mexico, the United States, and Canada. People who favored the agreement believed that the demand for American products in Mexico and Canada would rise and that more American workers would have to be hired to produce the extra exports.

Ross Perot, on the other hand, thought that the United States would lose a significant number of jobs if NAFTA passed. With fewer restrictions in place, he believed that manufacturing companies in this country would move their factories to Mexico. The minimum wage in Mexico is the equivalent of only $.58 an hour—compared to $4.25 an hour in the United States. So employers are able to spend much less on salaries that are paid to workers south of the U.S. border.

In his late 1993 book *Save Your Job, Save Our Country,* Perot reported that there were 1,300 U.S. companies that already operated 2,200 factories in Mexico. Employed in those plants were 500,000 Mexican workers. If those same companies had remained in this country, 500,000 Americans might have held those jobs. Perot said over and over that passage of the agreement would cause "a giant sucking sound of jobs heading south."[1]

Many organized labor unions also believed that NAFTA would reduce the already shrinking number of jobs available in the United States. During the 1980s many companies found that their products could be made at a lower cost by workers in countries such as Thailand and Sri Lanka. As many as two million U.S. jobs were lost after firms set up manufacturing operations overseas.

Those in favor of NAFTA argued that the jobs are moving out of this country anyway and they might just as well move to Mexico, who is our close neighbor. Proponents believed that certain terms of the agreement would force Mexican companies to raise their minimum hourly wages and improve working conditions in their factories. That in turn would improve the standard of living for the workers in Mexico so that they would have more money to spend on American products.

Supporters of the trade agreement also believed that if working conditions and wages were improved in Mexico, fewer citizens of that country would come to America illegally in search of a better way of life. Taxpayers in the U.S. pay the bill for illegal immigrants when they are provided with health care and welfare benefits and when their children are enrolled in public schools. If the standard of living in Mexico improved, maybe many of the immigrants would choose to remain at home in their own country.

Some people who opposed NAFTA believed that the illegal drug problem would only get worse if free trade were allowed. They were afraid that all of the extra trucks that would be needed to carry goods back and forth across the border would provide an excellent hiding place for smuggled narcotics. Supporters of the pact thought that the drug problem would actually decrease, because law enforcement agencies in the two countries would work together more closely and cooperate better.

Protection of the environment was another issue that divided many people on the NAFTA issue. The United States has strict laws to protect the environment. There are regulations about what factories can dump into the waterways and what they can emit into the air. Toxic chemicals must be disposed of according to set rules, and fines are assessed for failure to comply with the pollution laws.

In an effort to clean our air, cars that are driven in America must be equipped with emission-control devices and must run on unleaded gasoline. Mexico has very few laws that are designed to protect the environment. The country is poor and struggles to keep its people fed. Pollution laws have not been a high priority.

Those who opposed NAFTA worried that our air and water quality standards would be lowered as we worked more closely with Mexico. Proponents of the agreement argued that the pact would force Mexico to adopt tougher laws regarding the environment. Then maybe the country's air quality would improve and polluted rivers such as the Rio Grande would be cleaner.

As the deadline for passage of the agreement drew nearer, Ross Perot became more and more vocal in his criticism. Throughout the late summer and early fall of 1993, he spent almost every weekend at rallies around the country, urging people to help defeat NAFTA. He made the rounds of the television talk shows and wrote editorials that appeared in many newspapers.

While Perot was airing his views about the accord, President Clinton was joined by former Presidents Jimmy Carter, Gerald Ford, and George Bush in Washington, D.C. They were there to offer support while Clinton signed a NAFTA side agreements package.

After the signing Carter said, "Unfortunately, in our

country now, we have a demagogue who has unlimited financial resources and who is extremely careless with the truth who is preying on the fears and the uncertainties of the American public."[2]

When asked to respond to the charge Perot said, "Jimmy Carter is a good man. He cannot have read NAFTA."[3]

Just about a week before the House of Representatives was due to vote on NAFTA, Vice President Al Gore and Ross Perot agreed to debate the issue on television. CNN's *Larry King Live* show was the setting for the ninety-minute face-off on November 9, 1993. Early in the debate Gore took the offensive and attempted to discredit Perot as a wealthy businessman whose enterprises would stand to lose money if NAFTA passed.[4]

Vice President Gore stressed that the United States needed to be a part of the global economy and the world's largest trading partnership. He said that under the NAFTA agreement more American workers would be hired to produce goods for the new consumers in Mexico and Canada. Perot countered by saying that the country of Mexico was too poor to have as a trading partner. "People who can't make anything, can't buy anything," said Perot.[5]

NAFTA passed the House vote with a comfortable 234–200 margin on November 17, 1993. Three days later the Senate also approved the trade agreement by a

On the cable TV show, *Larry King Live,* Vice President Al Gore and
Ross Perot debated the NAFTA issue.

vote of 61–38. The trade agreement went into effect on January 1, 1994. Despite losing the NAFTA debate, Perot has said that he plans to continue touring the country to address issues that concern him—issues such as government reform and President Clinton's health care plan.

As Perot traveled around the country giving speeches about NAFTA he also encouraged people to join United We Stand, America. Early in 1994 UWSA held a National Leadership Conference in Dallas, Texas. During 1993 UWSA was organized in all fifty states, and each of the newly formed state organizations sent an elected chairperson and director to the conference. Their job was to help create a set of objectives that would govern the activities of UWSA during 1994.

National issues that the group wanted to study included health care reform, a balanced budget amendment, and term limits for elected officials. On the local level, delegates to the conference planned to mount a membership drive and improve communication among UWSA state organizations.

Ross Perot said to those attending the Dallas meeting, "You are now a very effective force in the country and you have created a certain amount of trauma by your presence. Both political parties are dedicated to see that you go away. We're not going away. We're going to grow."[6]

In addition to his work with UWSA, Ross Perot has

taken an interest in the health problems that plague some of the veterans of the 1991 Persian Gulf War. Several hundred of the veterans of that war have suffered from unexplained illnesses, including rashes, nausea, joint pain, fatigue, and hair loss. The U.S. government has been slow to react to their complaints and to provide adequate treatment. Perot established a toll-free number for the ailing veterans to call so that the extent of their problems could be documented and evaluated.

Ross Perot has also launched a campaign in opposition to President Clinton's proposed health care plan. In a speech at the American College of Cardiology Convention on March 14, 1994, Perot urged physicians to organize nationwide to formulate a health care plan that would be called "Put Patients First." He pledged $1 million to help finance the effort.[7]

As the months pass and the 1996 elections get closer, what does the future hold for Ross Perot? When he is asked about a possible presidential race in 1996, he refuses to comment. He won't reveal the number of UWSA members either, so no one can accurately measure his real power. One thing is certain though—Ross Perot probably won't ride into the sunset anytime soon. He may ride off a little way, but it will probably be just so he can get his bearings before he jumps into the fray again.

The historians will probably look back one day and pass judgment on the life of Ross Perot. They will no doubt find little to criticize about his personal life. He appears to have been a good husband and father who loves his family. It is hard to predict how historians will view Perot's political activities. What they can't disagree about is the fact that he got a large number of people involved in the workings of government.

The addition of Perot to the slate of candidates in the 1992 presidential race introduced a new element into the contest. A lot of people tuned in to watch the "infomercials" and debates because they just didn't know what Perot would say next. Ross Perot was fun to watch and he injected a shot of humor into some otherwise pretty dull proceedings. He talked about complicated topics in an uncomplicated manner.

Then an unusual consequence occurred. Some people who had not had much interest in politics before, started paying closer attention to the issues. Many saw that if enough interested citizens joined together, they could make an impact on the decision-making process in Washington, D.C. Even those who had no intention of voting for Perot could see the effect. Ross Perot and his enthusiastic volunteer movement gave a new sense of power to many people. No longer did they have to just sit back and take it. Now American citizens knew that petitions and phone calls and letters could make a difference—no matter what party they belonged to.

Americans were examining issues such as the federal budget, health care, and NAFTA with a new understanding. They were discussing politics over the dinner table and making their children aware of current events. Those same children will be the leaders of tomorrow. The more they know about the country that they call home, the better the country will be.

Whatever else the historians decide about Ross Perot, they can't deny that he helped to generate a renewed interest in the federal government and in many of the important issues that face America as the country moves toward the twenty-first century.

Chronology

1930—Born on June 27 in Texarkana, Texas

1943—Earns an Eagle Scout badge at age thirteen

1949—Enters United States Naval Academy on June 27

1953—Graduates from United States Naval Academy

1953—Serves aboard USS *Sigourney*
-1955

1955—Serves aboard USS *Leyte*
-1957

1956—Marries Margot Birmingham on September 15

1957—Goes to work for IBM in Dallas, Texas

1958—Son Ross, Jr. born

1960—Daughter Nancy born

1962—Founds Electronic Data Systems (EDS)

1964—Daughter Suzanne born

1968—EDS goes public; Perot becomes a billionaire; daughter Carolyn born

1969—Tries to take Christmas dinner to the POWs in Vietnam; founds United We Stand

1970—Perot family moves to twenty-two-acre estate in Dallas; attempts a second delivery to POWs in Vietnam

1971—Daughter Katherine born

1979—Helps free two EDS employees from Iranian prison; named chairman of Governor's Texas War on Drugs Committee

1984—Heads Texas Governor's Task Force on
–1985 Education

1984—General Motors (GM) buys EDS

1986—GM buys out Perot for $700 million

1992—Announces bid for presidency on March 18;
       drops out of presidential race on July 16;
       re-enters presidential race on October 1;
       publishes *United We Stand*

1993—Begins United We Stand, America on January
       11; publishes *Not for Sale at Any Price* and *Save
       Your Job, Save Our Country*

Chapter Notes

Chapter 1

1. "The Wild Card," *Newsweek*, April 27, 1992, p. 28.

2. Ross Perot, *United We Stand* (New York: Hyperion, 1992), p. 36.

3. Ken Herman, "Clinton: A New Beginning," *Houston Post*, November 4, 1992, p. A11.

Chapter 2

1. Ken Gross, *Ross Perot: The Man Behind the Myth* (New York: Random House, 1992), p. 20.

2. "Ross Perot: Dallas Crusader," *Newsweek*, April 13, 1970, p. 69.

3. Tony Freemantle, "Perot's Hometown Not Surprised," *Houston Chronicle*, June 21, 1992, p. A1.

4. John W. Kirshon, ed., *Chronicle of America* (New York: Chronicle Publications), p. 699.

5. Freemantle, p. A1.

6. Ibid.

Chapter 3

1. Todd Mason, *Perot: An Unauthorized Biography* (Homewood, Ill.: Dow Jones-Irwin, 1990), p. 30.

2. Ken Gross, *Ross Perot: The Man Behind the Myth* (New York: Random House, 1992), p. 44.

3. Barbara Hordern, "Lady in Waiting," *Ladies' Home Journal*, September 1992, p. 172.

4. "The Man and the Myth," *Newsweek*, June 15, 1992, p. 21.

5. "Perot Sought 2-Years-Early Exit From Navy, Documents Indicate," *Houston Chronicle*, May 15, 1992, p. A19.

6. Sandra McElwaine, "Exclusive! We Visit Margot Perot," *Good Housekeeping*, September 1992, p. 268.

Chapter 4

1. "Ross Perot: Dallas Crusader," *Newsweek*, April 13, 1970, p. 69.

2. David Remnick, "True-Life Adventures of H. Ross Perot," *Reader's Digest*, September 1987, p. 169.

3. Todd Mason, *Perot: An Unauthorized Biography* (Homewood, Ill.: Dow Jones-Irwin, 1990), p. 36.

4. John W. Kirshon, ed., *Chronicle of America* (New York: Chronicle Publications), p. 732.

Chapter 5

1. Todd Mason, *Perot: An Unauthorized Biography* (Homewood, Ill.: Dow Jones-Irwin, 1990), p. 43.

2. Tony Chiu, *Ross Perot: In His Own Words* (New York: Warner Books, 1992), p. 13.

3. "Ross Perot's Crusade," *Business Week*, October 6, 1986, p. 63.

4. Chiu, p. 11.

5. Peter Elkind, "Can Ross Perot Save America?" *Texas Monthly*, December 1988, p. 193.

6. Ken Gross, *Ross Perot: The Man Behind the Myth* (New York: Random House, 1992), p. 111.

Chapter 6

1. "Money Talks," *Newsweek*, December 8, 1969, p. 58.

2. David Remnick, "True-Life Adventures of H. Ross Perot," *Reader's Digest*, September 1987, p. 171.

3. John W. Kirshon, ed., *Chronicle of America* (New York: Chronicle Publications), p. 847.

4. Ross Ramsey, "Perot Says It's Time for Action, Not Talk," *Houston Chronicle*, May 10, 1992, p. A1.

5. Ken Gross, *Ross Perot: The Man Behind the Myth* (New York: Random House, 1992), p. 161.

6. Roy Rowan, "The World According to Perot," *Life*, February 1988, p. 68.

7. "Ross Perot's Problem Child," *Newsweek*, February 18, 1974, p. 71.

8. Ibid.

Chapter 7

1. "Perot's Impossible Mission," *Newsweek*, March 5, 1979, p. 48.

2. Ken Follett, *On Wings of Eagles* (New York: Penguin Books, 1984), p. 166.

3. "Perot's Impossible Mission," p. 47.

4. Roy Rowan, "The World According to Perot," *Life*, February 1988, p. 67.

Chapter 8

1. Todd Mason, *Perot: An Unauthorized Biography* (Homewood, Ill.: Dow Jones-Irwin, 1990), p. 125.

2. Nick Thimmesch, "Ross Perot: Computer Commando," *Saturday Evening Post*, April 1983, p. 96.

3. Ross Ramsey, "Perot Says It's Time for Action, Not Talk," *Houston Chronicle*, May 10, 1992, p. A18.

4. Mason, p. 126.

5. Joseph Nocera, "Will the Real Ross Perot Please Stand Up?" *Business Week*, May 21, 1990, p. 23.

6. Roy Rowan, "The World According to Perot," *Life*, February 1988, p. 66.

7. "Ross Perot's Crusade," *Business Week*, October 6, 1986, p. 61.

8. David Remnick, "True-Life Adventures of H. Ross Perot," *Reader's Digest*, September 1987, p. 172.

9. "Marital Spat," *Time*, December 8, 1986, p. 63.

10. "Peace For a Price at GM," *Time*, December 15, 1986, p. 51.

11. Rowan, p. 66.

Chapter 9

1. Barbara Hordern, "Lady in Waiting," *Ladies' Home Journal*, September 1992, p. 172.

2. Hamilton Jordan, "On Perot's Team—Why I Split with the Democrats," *Houston Chronicle*, June 9, 1992, p. A17.

3. Edward Rollins, "Working for Perot—Why I Split with the GOP," *Houston Chronicle*, June 9, 1992, p. A17.

4. Elizabeth Gleick, "Perot's Hidden Assets," *People Weekly*, June 15, 1992, p. 106.

Chapter 10

1. "Ross Perot's Crusade," *Business Week*, October 6, 1986, p. 62.

2. Thomas Ferguson, "The Lost Crusade of Ross Perot," *The Nation*, August 17/24, 1992, p. 172.

3. Alan Farnham, "And Now, Here's the Man Himself," *Fortune*, June 15, 1992, p. 68.

4. Norm Brewer, "Rudman, Tsongas Unveil Plan to Eliminate Deficit," *Houston Post*, September 21, 1993, p. A1.

5. Martin Gross, *The Government Racket* (New York: Bantam Books, 1992), p. 240.

6. "Perot Quest for Petition Signatures to End at State Capitol Today," *Houston Chronicle*, May 11, 1992, p. A10.

7. "Superhero," *Newsweek*, November/December 1992, p. 76.

8. Walter Shapiro, "President Perot?" *Time*, May 25, 1992, p. 27, 28.

9. Laurence Barrett, "Perot Takes a Walk," *Time*, July 27, 1992, p. 33.

10. "The Strange Tales of Mr. Barnes," *Newsweek*, November 9, 1992, p. 24.

11. "It Was Take No Prisoners Time at the Debate," *Houston Post*, October 12, 1992, p. A10.

12. Christopher George, "Perot and Con," *The Washington Monthly*, June 1993, p. 40.

Chapter 11

1. "Election '92," *Time*, November 16, 1992, p. 19.

2. Howard Fineman, "The Torch Passes," *Newsweek*, November/December 1992, p. 9.

3. Eric Grafstrom, "Area Code 202 is Busy," *United We Stand America Newsletter*, Summer 1993, p. 14.

4. Christopher George, "Perot and Con," *The Washington Monthly*, June 1993, p. 38.

5. Gloria Borger and Jerry Buckley, "Perot Keeps Going and Going . . ." *U.S. News & World Report*, May 17, 1993, p. 44.

Chapter 12

1. Bennett Roth, "Foley: NAFTA Vote Will Be Close," *Houston Chronicle*, August 23, 1993, p. A2.

2. John Gravois, "Clinton Signs NAFTA Side Accords—With a Little Help," *Houston Post*, September 15, 1993, p. A1.

3. "Clinton Says NAFTA Will Start Export Boom," *Houston Post*, September 16, 1993, p. 12.

4. "Beware of Veeps Bearing Gifts," *Newsweek*, November 22, 1993, p. 8.

5. William F. Buckley, "Perot vs. Gore," *National Review*, December 13, 1993, p. 70.

6. Shari Guthrie, "National Membership Drive Kicks Off," *United We Stand America Newsletter*, Spring 1994, p. 1.

7. "1994 UWSA National Leadership Conference," *United We Stand America Newsletter*, Spring 1994, p. 12.

Further Reading

Dolan, Edward. *MIA: Missing in Action.* New York: Franklin Watts, 1989.

Farnham, Alan. "And Now, Here's the Man Himself." *Fortune.* June 15, 1992, pp. 68–74.

Follett, Ken. *On Wings of Eagles.* New York: Penguin Books, 1983.

Gross, Ken. *Ross Perot: The Man Behind the Myth.* New York: Random House, 1992.

"The Man and the Myth." *Newsweek.* June 15, 1992, pp. 20–27.

Perot, Ross. *Not for Sale at Any Price.* New York: Hyperion, 1993.

Perot, Ross, and Pat Choate. *Save Your Job, Save Our Country.* New York: Hyperion, 1993.

Perot, Ross. *United We Stand.* New York: Hyperion, 1992.

Rowan, Roy. "The World According to Ross Perot." *Life.* February 1988, pp. 65–70.

Seal, Mark. "Retro Man." *Esquire.* July 1992, pp. 85–88.

"The Wild Card." *Newsweek.* April 27, 1992, pp. 21–27.

Index